Lasallian Spirituality Today

December 2023
www.lasallianresources.org

Authors:
Valère Adonsou, FSC (*Ivory Coast*)
Adriana Bolaños (*México*)
Óscar Elizalde (*Colombia*)
Jill Gowdie (*Australia*)
Julia Mayer (*Austria*)
Prita Nambbiar (*Malaysia*)
Luis Bolívar, FSC
(*Secretariat for Formation*)
George Van Grieken, FSC
(*Lasallian Research and Resources*)
Heather Ruple
(*Secretariat for Association*)
Paco Chiva, FSC
(*Secretariat for Association*)

Special thanks to the religious leaders who participated in the panel session - in Rome - on spirituality in other religions: Guglielmo Doryu Cappelli (Buddhism-Zen), Mohamed Ben Mohamed (Islam), Jacov Di Segni (Judaism).

Collaborators:
Ilaria Iadeluca
(*Communications Services – Generalate*)
Routhier Gilles (*Canada*)
Paulo Dullius, FSC
(*Secretariat for Formation*)

Cover, back cover and graphic design: Jo Millea
(*Great Britain*)

Translators:
Antoine Salinas, FSC
Agustin Ranchal, FSC

This is a RELAN version of the original February 2023 Institute publication.

December, 2023
Lasallian Resource Center.
www.lasallianresources.org

Index

Introduction: 5

1. Graphic of Lasallian Spirituality 7
2. Development of Lasallian Spirituality 8
   Spirituality 8
   Lasallian Spirituality 10
   Lasallian Mission 12
   Lasallian School /Ministry 13
   Lasallian Education 14

Lasallian Spirituality Overview 17
   An Incarnational Spirituality 22
   The Lasallian Vocational Journey 24

The Dynamics of Lasallian Spirituality 28
   The Holy Presence of God 29
   Trust in God's Ways 30
   Passion for the Mission 37
   Together and by Association 41

Where Is Lasallian Spirituality Found? 44
   In a Distinctive Kind of Education 44
   In a Distinctive Kind of Educator 47

Living Lasallian Spirituality 49
   The Personal 49
   The Relational 52
   The Professional 53

Conclusion 54

3. Horizons of Lasallian Spirituality 56
   Educators for Wisdom 57
   Witnesses to Transcendence 58
   Promoters of Dialogue 59
   Models in Accompaniment 60
   Agents of Transformation 61

Footnotes 62

Introduction:

Dear Lasallians,

Over the past few years, the Secretariat for Association has held virtual visits and meetings with educators, teachers, Brothers, volunteers, and other members of the Lasallian Family from all over the world. From these encounters we hear the call to deepen our spirituality.

With the leadership of the Lasallian Research and Resources Service we conducted an international survey and published a Report[1] on each District's efforts to promote Lasallian Spirituality, and what programs and resources were being used. To respond to some of the findings of that research, we created an International Think Tank to work on providing a better understanding of Lasallian Spirituality within the Lasallian Family.

You hold in your hands the fruit of two-year-ongoing work of this group. We have been meeting once a month since 2020, by videoconference, due to the constraints of the pandemic. We have shared together and worked in person for 7 days in Rome in July 2022. Our contribution to Lasallian Spirituality includes an animated graphic (which can be a good pedagogical resource for intuitive and quick access to Lasallian Spirituality); a brief but systematic explanation of its components; and a proposal of horizons (which will allow us to direct our energies in the coming years).

We hope that this initiative, along with others[2], can help in the formation and development of Lasallian Spirituality in your Districts and educational works. Please do not hesitate to share with us any initiative that will help us to live our spirituality more deeply: **association@lasalle.org**. We remain at your service.

Live Jesus in our hearts!

Ms. Heather Ruple and Br. Paco Chiva, FSC
Co-Secretaries for Association

Br. George Van Grieken, FSC
Lasallian Research and Resources

Rome, October 2022

1. Graphic of Lasallian Spirituality

2. Development of Lasallian Spirituality

Spirituality

1. Spirituality is "a dimension of human existence that can be expressed either within or independently of a religious tradition. It is a person's way of being, thinking, choosing, and acting in the world according to that person's ultimate values."[3]

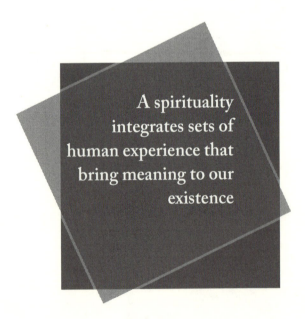

A spirituality integrates sets of human experience that bring meaning to our existence

2. A spirituality integrates sets of human experience that bring meaning to our existence, because "everything is connected",[4] opening up different forms of relationship with transcendence. It offers an invitation to touch realities that lie beyond us, to reach out to all life and to the Creator. A spirituality calls for a coherence between our inner and outer lives. "The fundamental call is to be fully human in our love and to contribute with our whole being towards the humanization of our societies."[5] In education, Church documents affirm that "the integral formation of the human person, which is the purpose of education, includes the development of all the human faculties of the students, together with preparation for professional life, formation of ethical and social awareness, becoming aware of the transcendental, and religious education."[6]

Lasallian Spirituality

3. Lasallian spirituality is a way of being in the world "by which persons seek to integrate their lives through cooperation with God in the ministry of human and Christian education, especially with those who are poor, according to the vision of John Baptist de La Salle."[7]

4. Lasallian spirituality animates a "charism", a God-given grace for the world that is expressed in a specific way of life or ministry. The Lasallian charism is lived out through a "spirit of faith that gives rise personally and communally to a spirit of zeal for salvation of the young, especially those who are poor. This spirit draws people into a community that inspires educators to provide a human and Christian education to the young, especially the poor."[8]

5. Lasallian spirituality is a holistic educational spirituality that integrates all of one's experiences. It is a spirituality of dialogue, reciprocity, and complementarity by which educational relationships become a means of encountering the deeper natures of ourselves and the world at large. Lasallian spirituality is open to different forms of relationship; with others, with transcendence, and ultimately with the mystery of God. It is "in the mystery and majesty of the personal that God lives.[9]

Lasallian Mission

6. The Lasallian mission developed as a courageous and creative response to the educational needs of children of artisans and the poor in France in the 17th century. Centuries of experience have advanced and refined major themes of this Lasallian mission: dwelling in the Presence of God, growing in the light of the Word of God, living by the spirit of faith and zeal as part of the Church's educational outreach to the marginalized, and experiencing a shared mission in community, together and by Association. Today, it is our creative fidelity to these and similar fundamental ideals that ensures its ongoing vitality.

7. There can be no Lasallian mission without people who live a Lasallian spirituality. The Lasallian spirituality that drives the mission is empowered and shaped by the character, charism, and vision of St. John Baptist de La Salle and the first Brothers. Their shared experiences and collaboration shaped their charismatic path and established the Institute. It is deeply rooted in Jesus Christ and the Gospel. Further primary historical sources for Lasallian spirituality include the Catholic heritage, our Institute's founding story, the Gospel journey of St. John Baptist de La Salle, and the long-line of Brothers who dedicated their lives to its realization. Finally, the Lasallian Family has contributed to the development and incarnation of spirituality in multiple cultures and in dialogue with other spiritualties.

Lasallian School / Ministry

8. The Lasallian school is part of the educational movement initiated by St. John Baptist de La Salle and continued by those who followed him. A Lasallian school lives out its identity through the values and priorities on which it is based, the character of its educational community, the nature of its organizational climate, and the consistent practices that it demonstrates.

9. A Lasallian school is part of the Catholic tradition of educational ministry. It invites students "to consider a spiritual grounding for their lives in the world that might make their lives a little more meaningful, worthwhile, purposeful, ethical, and might sustain them in the tough times."[10] A Lasallian school provides students with an academically rigorous, competent, and capable education that prepares them to make a living, but it also prepares them to have a life grounded in some kind of faith perspective as they engage in the world. "The Catholic school sets out to be a school for the human person and of the human person."[11]

Lasallian Education

10. Today the Lasallian Educational Mission has diverse expressions in varied works and ministries across the globe. There is a unity in this diversity. Both this unity and this diversity are celebrated. The source of its unity is in its Christian identity, the spiritual journey of St. John Baptist de La Salle, and the educational tradition that bears his name. The strength of its diversity lies in the breadth of its multi-cultural and multi- religious reality, an inclusive community that values each person, and supportive relationship at all levels of the educational experience.

11. Contemporary Lasallian spirituality asks: "How can our deep gift meet the world's deep need today?"[12] Given the realities of the contemporary world, especially in education, this requires constant attention. What do these students need? What do today's educators need to better understand, appreciate, and engage their Lasallian heritage and spirituality? A living Lasallian spirituality never stops interpreting and describing itself, specifying and adapting the expression of its core elements for each new generation, enriched by their insights, experiences, and conversations. This is how Lasallian spirituality thrives.

12. The Lasallian world is marked by the diversity of its cultural and religious experiences, and by the unity of its shared identity. Differences in country, culture, religious or spiritual traditions, economic status, gender, etc. have never deterred children, adolescents, young adults, and adults from claiming La Salle as part of a shared identity. This identity arises from the appropriation, integration, and sharing of common educational principles and emphases that are essential to the Lasallian heritage. Distinctive elements of other religious traditions can also contribute to the religious understanding and spiritual traditions that are essential to Lasallian education. While everyone may not fully embrace the entirety of Lasallian identity or its spirituality, all will know that they are valued within its circle.

13. The best way to learn about Lasallian spirituality is to be part of an authentic Lasallian educational community. This means interacting with teachers, students, and administrators; visiting classes, athletic events, and other activities; participating in its interpersonal and community dynamics.

Education is a human learning journey, a lifelong activity, an abiding interest for all. Lasallian education permeates the human learning journey with priorities, perspectives, and deeply held convictions that bear a living history, a worldwide identity, and a vision of what education is able to be. The pedagogical approach of Lasallian educators, the administrative styles and priorities, and the organizational climate and the values of the educational institution best demonstrate its Lasallian Catholic character.

"We believe that another world is possible, and that education is a fundamental force for building it. Our educational perspective aims to build societies where peace, equity, social justice, civic participation, the raising up of common dreams, and a respect for freedom and difference are possible. We visibly demonstrate our commitment to the building up of a more democratic and just society, as well as our option for an integral and sustainable human development that benefits everyone. To educate for peace is to educate for justice and solidarity."[13]

Lasallian Spirituality Overview

14. Lasallian spirituality expresses a way for educators to encounter God's Holy Presence with and for those entrusted to their care. "Because you are ambassadors and ministers of Jesus Christ in the work that you do, you must act as representing Jesus Christ himself. He wants your disciples to see him in you and receive your instructions as if he were giving them to them. [2 Cor. 5:20]"[14]

15. Three traditional components of Lasallian spirituality are faith, zeal, and community. Lasallian education is animated by an interior dimension (faith) and by an exterior expression (zeal) that are engaged within an active educational community. It is a spirit that is focused on education and on educators who are wholly dedicated to students, "those entrusted to their care," and who pursue three levels of engagement – the personal vocational, the communal relational, and the ministerial professional.

16. The "spirit" that John Baptist de La Salle identified as "The spirit of the Institute" intrinsically combines "faith" and "zeal." This integration of a deep trust in God with an active passion for ministry is something that he came to understand as a single reality: "Do not distinguish between the duties of your state and what pertains to your salvation and perfection. You can be sure that you will never achieve your salvation more certainly and acquire greater perfection than by fulfilling well the duties of your state, provided you do so in view of the will of God."[15]

17. This "spirit of faith & zeal" is expressed in and through the community. "Union in a community is a precious gem, which is why our Lord so often recommended it to his apostles before he died. If we lose this, we lose everything. Preserve it with care, therefore, if you want your community to survive."[16] Community is how Lasallian spirituality comes to life and how it is supported and sustained. It is the engine of Lasallian education.

18. It is important to observe that Jesus Christ's person, mission, and message are the source from which Lasallian principles and processes emerged, and the core values of our Lasallian spiritual tradition come from the Christian Gospel and the Catholic heritage. At the same time, there

is a profoundly human dimension that underlies all religious capacities. Christian virtues are first and centrally profoundly human virtues, and as such they are within the scope of all human experience. For De La Salle, for the Brothers throughout Lasallian history, and for a majority of Lasallians today, this Christian dimension bears unique and significant implications for how Lasallian spirituality is understood and lived out.

19. The foundational convictions of Lasallian ministries have a universal dimension that promotes both human and Christian growth, and they lead us to care for and preserve all that is profoundly human. In today's plural and interreligious world, Lasallian spirituality also finds sources and resources in the sacred texts of other religions and in their traditions. Lasallian spirituality, active and alive in the world of education, welcomes all that advances the capacity to appreciate a "holy presence" and promotes the good of those entrusted to our care.[17] This underlies the importance of the ecumenical and interreligious dimension of Lasallian spirituality.

20. Lasallian spirituality is essentially an incarnational spirituality that is lived out in community through individual vocational journeys. Three primary dynamics shape those Lasallian journeys and result in a distinctive kind of education and a distinctive kind of educator. Lasallian educators pursue a Lasallian vocation that is permeated by personal, relational, and professional dynamics that draw from Lasallian roots and from its Catholic heritage. In the rest of this document, all of these elements will be described in more detail so that they may be better understood and engaged for the benefit of those entrusted to our care.

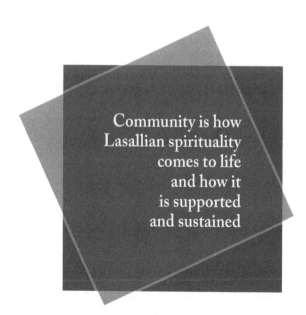

Community is how Lasallian spirituality comes to life and how it is supported and sustained

An Incarnational Spirituality

21. John Baptist de La Salle's life was transformed by a humble and deeply incarnational engagement with God's presence in all the events of his life. This never left him. God was present in all the circumstances, decisions, and challenges in his life. His dying words reflect this total orientation: "I adore all the ways God has acted in my life."[18] He was a mystic in action, sensitive to the deep, broad, and permanent presence of God in our lives.[19]

22. "Given that the fundamental starting point for our Lasallian educational spirituality is its incarnational quality, it would be true to say that each of us embodies and gives expression to that identity and vitality."[20] Lasallian spirituality is an incarnated spirituality that sees the school as a place of salvation, a place that is both sign and promise that God lives with us and through us. Its realization requires a gaze of faith, a long loving look into, behind, and beyond the daily realities we encounter, quietly helping those entrusted to our care discover purpose and meaning as we teach, counsel, or guide them.

23. The incarnational dimension of Lasallian identity encompasses a habitual movement toward the transcendent, a passion for education in all its rich complexity, and a community with shared Lasallian mission priorities. All Lasallians, in their own way, embody these elements of Lasallian identity in their ministry.

> St. John Baptist de La Salle was a mystic in action, sensitive to the deep, broad, and permanent presence of God in our lives

The Lasallian Vocational Journey

24. A vocation is a calling and a disposition to follow a particular path of life. When we speak of the Lasallian vocation, we speak of the calling to be part of the circle of lifelong educators and lifelong learners who see learning and teaching as a holy endeavor that is deeply relational, centered on teaching the minds, touching the hearts, and transforming the lives of those entrusted to their care. These are "true mediators for their students" who "strive to promote the development of interiority and competence."[21] "Integrity, example, depth, vision, respect, tenderness, ardent zeal, faith and hope will always be the virtues that will characterize the upright teacher's ability to mediate."[22]

25. The means of engaging Lasallian spirituality and developing a Lasallian vocation aligns with several foundational perspectives:

- All are invited to become part of this educational heritage in light of their own experience and perspective. Each person must determine why and how they are attracted to it, and how they may best integrate this charism as part of their lives.

- The Lasallian charism animates both multicultural and multireligious contexts. Hence, Lasallian spirituality is called to dialogue with a variety of cultures and spiritualities, informed by the ecumenical and interreligious perspective advocated by the Church and guided by its own historical heritage.
- Ways of becoming more engaged in the Lasallian charism are individually shaped, community supported, and experientially assessed. They must align with the outlines of one's personal and professional growth, neither undermining nor superseding their integrity.
- Helpful resources provide a larger framework for understanding and approaching Lasallian "formation" and personal growth, along with ways of describing likely levels, objectives, activities, and goals. *Lasallian Formation for Mission: A Pilgrim's Handbook* and Circular 475, *From Hope to Commitment: Understanding Lasallian Vocations*, are the most contemporary resources.
- The vocation of the Brothers "according to our Founder and according to Vatican II, is to make the loving and saving presence of Christ a visible and effective reality in the world of education and among the young."[23]

26. Lasallian formation is "a process of interiorizing the constitutive elements of Lasallian identity."[24] It involves a multifaceted, lifelong, intentional pursuit of coming to know, understand, and practice the essential and dynamic dimensions of what it means to be associated in the Lasallian charism. Genuine Lasallian formation is rooted in accompaniment, "walking with others on the journey, sharing wisdom and insights learned from the Lasallian pilgrimage",[25] and it results in the development of deeper spirituality, a deeper belonging, and a renewed commitment to the vocation of a Lasallian educator.

27. St. John Baptist de La Salle provides the most helpful description of the Lasallian vocational journey. He wrote that God "who guides all things with wisdom and serenity, whose way it is not to force the inclinations of persons, willed to commit me entirely to the development of the schools. He did this in an imperceptible way and over a long period of time, so that one commitment led to another in a way that

I did not foresee in the beginning."[26] It was the daily events, the personal encounters, the deliberate conversations with his Brothers and others that brought Lasallian spirituality to life. And it was the concrete practices in his personal life, in the Brothers communities, and in the schools that gave expression to that spirituality. This also applies to those who wish to pursue this Lasallian vocational journey today – no forced inclinations, a long period of time, one commitment leading to another, an almost imperceptible advancement, and the pursuit of specific spiritual practices.

"Vocation is a life-long process and it is not reduced to the one individual call. Rather, it is seen as a succession of calls and responses, a dialogue in freedom between God and each human being, which is concretized in a mission that must be discovered continuously in the different stages of life and in relation to new realities. The fundamental call is to be fully human in our love and to contribute with our whole being towards the humanization of our societies."[27]

The Dynamics of Lasallian Spirituality

28. "Lasallian identity and spirituality find their origins in the practice of reflecting on daily experiences to recognize God's loving presence and action. This dynamic interaction touches the hearts of Lasallians and moves them to become co-workers with God in the mission."[28] It is a dynamic that comes from the perspective of faith, which Scripture defines as "the substance of things hoped for, the assurance of things not seen."[29] Such faith has strong echoes in each authentic educational encounter where the "things hoped for" are mediated by teachers who are caring, practical, patient, and kind. (1 Cor. 13)

29. We participate in the Lasallian mission when we remember that the "Holy Presence of God" embraces all

that we say, do, or are in our ministry of Lasallian education or our Lasallian educational project. "That which is specifically Lasallian has to do with a style, a methodology and a tradition that is made explicit in a rich, constructive, and personalized educational relationship. This educational relationship is inspired by a spirituality that is based on faith, fraternity and ardent zeal."[30]

The Holy Presence of God

30. The prayer that begins Lasallian activities provides a starting hope and a defining end: "Let us remember that we are in the Holy Presence of God."[31] Some form of this prayer is used each day in Lasallian schools, communities, and ministries throughout the world. From the earliest times, this prayer "will help the teachers to recollect themselves and recall the presence of God; it will serve to accustom the students to think of God from time to time and to offer God all their actions, and to draw upon themselves God's blessing."[32] In very few words, and with habitual frequency, it is a statement that invites intentional reflection, renewed awareness, and a change in perspective. The words are the setting of the jewel of that shared silence. This central Lasallian prayer and invocation encapsulates an essential dimension of our Lasallian identity, mission, community, and charism. It invites us to do what we say and to live what we believe.

Trust in God's Ways

31. There is a basic level of trust that empowers all educational endeavors. Trust is the precondition for good relationships, for solidarity. Good teachers see beyond the initial character of those they teach. They bring new perspectives to perceived limitations. Where students see little talent, teachers see previously unrecognized possibilities. Where students see educational setbacks, teachers see new opportunities for growth. Where students see personal barriers, teachers see ways to overcome challenges. The best teachers gradually transform student perspectives such that students begin to appreciate their educational capacities and realize their agency in the educational process.

32. In the Lasallian educational context, this transformative dynamic is informed by a transcendent dimension that recognizes the active agency of God in the educational encounter. In his meditations, De La Salle describes how God is present in the teacher, the student, and the educational relationship.

33. Educators are like "good architects," "guardian angels," "cooperators" with Jesus Christ and his "ambassadors and ministers."[33] They mediate God's presence for students. "He wants your disciples to see him in you and receive your instructions as if he were giving them to them."[34] The educator is invited to adopt the example of Jesus the Teacher. "The nobility of the task to which teachers are called demands that, in imitation of Christ, the only Teacher, they reveal the Christian message not only by word but also by every gesture of their behavior."[35]

34. Students are endowed with a respect and honor that reaches far beyond the expected limits that society imposes.

"Regard the children whom God has entrusted to you as children of God."[36] They are "the living images of Jesus Christ," and teachers "should honor Jesus Christ in their person."[37] It is God who is brought to bear in the student.

"Recognize Jesus beneath the poor rags of the children whom you have to instruct. Adore Him in them."[38] The holy presence that is invoked in prayer is revealed in each educational encounter. Each student bears unique mysteries of depth and significance. "One of the essential foundations of Lasallian pedagogy is the knowledge that the teacher must have of each and every one of the students."[39]

35. Lasallian pedagogy places the educational relationship at the center of its activity. The educational relationship carries moral obligations for the holistic welfare of our students, including the spiritual dimension. "It is God himself who … gives you responsibility to provide for all their spiritual needs."[40]

There is much more to the Lasallian teaching encounter than the transmission of knowledge. It is a care of souls, which brings with it both a deeper responsibility and wider implications. "By taking upon yourselves the responsibility for their souls, you have, so to speak, offered to him soul for soul."[41] Such relationships have a transformative potential that touches hearts and carries an impact that extends throughout life.

36. The capacity to recognize the transcendent dimension in the educational encounter is something that is neither immediately obvious nor automatically sustained. De La

Salle's advocacy for prayer and meditation for those in the ministry of teaching was frequent, serious, and comprehensive. "It is your duty to go up to God every day in prayer to learn from him all that you must teach the children."[42] Habits of prayer and meditation benefit both educators and students, especially when these are informed and guided by De La Salle's meditations or other more contemporary resources that help us to better understand our vocation and educational ministry.

37. Interiority and an intentional awareness of transcendent dimensions of the educational encounter are accessible to everyone. They are part of our human identity. "Lasallians continuously discover that living the educational mission meaningfully opens up ways to spirituality and awareness of the very Presence of God found in different faith traditions. Br. Michel Sauvage called this 'endowing our life with mystical realism.' Belonging to the Lasallian Family means experiencing the Absolute daily, in meeting others, in our ordinary tasks, especially when we  discover the needs and talents of children and young people as well as our own."[43]

38. Scripture provides unique and special ways of learning about or encountering God. Education and Gospel teachings have defined Lasallian identity since the beginning. "From the origins of the Institute, this spirit of faith has been united with the spirit of zeal, with commitment and self-giving. ... Pope Francis reminds the Church: 'Spirit-filled evangelizers are evangelizers who pray and work. Mystical notions without a solid social and missionary outreach are of no help to evangelization, nor are dissertations or social or pastoral practices which lack a spirituality which can change hearts.'[44] An incarnated Christian spirituality always leads to commitments on behalf of children and young people most in need."[45] As we live the Gospel, we come to know the Gospel, and the "poor" become our teachers.

39. The "poor" have many faces today. Lasallian spirituality calls for the communication of God's love, the Good News, and advocacy for those in need, especially in the area of education. "Many children have poor or no education at all due to poverty, wars, migratory processes, social marginalization, epidemics, impossibility of access to new technologies, internal conflicts, racial or gender segregation, adolescent pregnancy, child labor and many other forms of exclusion."[46] It is our duty and privilege to educate those who are vulnerable, living in poverty or at the margins, bringing them into our midst and enabling them to pursue their dignity and full maturity as children of God. The Lasallian mission is an expression of the "preferential option for the poor"[47] in the world of education.

40. A Lasallian education for those on peripheries should equal, if not exceed, the excellence of education for others. "Poor education for the poor deprives them of access to the opportunities that their birth, surname or their social condition have denied them, thus perpetuating their marginalization and the conditions of misery in which many of them already live. Quality education is an engine of social mobility because it strengthens democracy, significantly reduces poverty and generates inclusion and equality."[48]

Passion for the Mission

41. A Gospel-based passion for education is the experienced manifestation of the life of the Holy Spirit within the Lasallian mission, God's creative presence in our midst. The "effects of the spirit of faith – Christian apostolic vision, action and passion – can be understood and lived only insofar as one responds to the illuminating, activating, and fortifying grace of the Spirit ... teaching, counseling, encouraging and inspiring the young in their Christian life. Apostolic prayer, catechetical instruction."[49] Pastoral vigilance and good example enable the Christian educator to accomplish this vital mission "with the pneumatic dynamism given by the Spirit to His ministers of the Word."[50]

42. The teachings of the Master, his life and mission, his option for the poor and excluded, his internalized values and priorities, his life-generating encounters, and his dedication to advancing the cause of God's reign to its ultimate consequences, are the basis for a spirituality of following Jesus. It is a particular way of relating to God the Father and of allowing oneself to be mobilized by the Holy Spirit. It is this Gospel, this "Good News," that motivates, energizes, and defines the Christian understanding and expression of De La Salle's original charism.

43. "John Baptist de La Salle was concerned with forming good citizens and good Christians, and so all those who are linked to Lasallian work strive to live the spirit of faith, and they associate with one another and are passionate about education."[51] Lasallian education has traditionally expressed its passion for education as the spirit of zeal, manifested through sustained programs of genuine quality. Administrators and educators demonstrate their character and priorities in how they serve all students. Likewise, "A competent Lasallian teacher masters his or her area of knowledge and knows how to transmit that knowledge to the students with proper respect and accompaniment, in addition to attending to administrative requirements."[52]

44. The Lasallian charism is expressed through Christian and human education that is "based on the nature of the human person, and therefore must take into account all of the physical and spiritual powers of each individual, along with the call of each one to be an active and creative agent in service to society."[53] Lasallian education, like other educational charisms in the Church, builds on and engages every deeply human capacity of the person. It lives out an integral humanism from a Christian context. "An integral education aims to gradually develop every capability of every student: his or her intellectual, physical, psychological, moral, and religious capacities."[54] The core values of this spiritual tradition come from the Gospel and have a universal dimension that promotes both human and Christian growth, promoting

> The core values of this spiritual tradition come from the Gospel and have a universal dimension that promotes both human and Christian growth

and witnessing everyday dialogue and unity. The Lasallian Family has joined Pope Francis in the *Global Compact on Education*, by which we commit to creating a global change of mentality through education, teaching students to overcome divisions and conflicts, and to promote hospitality, justice and peace.[55]

45. The Christian concept of the person "attributes to the human person the dignity of a child of God. ... It calls for the fullest development of all that is human."[56] While it is Christian in origin, a student-centered, effective, and efficient, Lasallian education accepts religious pluralism with respect and hope, acknowledging the nature of the human person. Lasallian and Church documents "emphasize the need for an educational philosophy built on a correct understanding of who the human person is."[57]

46. Numerous Lasallian saints, blesseds, and martyrs have given their lives for love of God, love of neighbor, and love of their students, and the same passion and commitment may be found among many living today. They demonstrate a spirituality of witness that puts into practice the values of the Gospel with joy and simplicity and nourish the credibility of a Christian life that may be lived with profound mysticism and prophetic action. They continue to inspire Lasallian educators today, silent witnesses to hard work, a passion for education, and a consistent personal life of prayer. As Pope Francis affirmed to the Brothers, "the Christian educator, in the school of Christ, is first of all a witness, and is a teacher to the extent that he/she is a witness".[58]

Together and by Association

47. Lasallian spirituality, based on the Trinity – the source of love, the expression of love, and the substance of love – is a relational, fraternal spirituality that enters into dialogue with God, with people, with oneself, and with creation. It welcomes the other through human encounters and an integral ecological awareness, thereby living a healthy relationship with the world and with one's neighbor. As Pope Francis has said, we "are called to become experts in the art of encounter (…). True encounter arises only from listening. This happens whenever we listen with the heart: people feel that they are being heard, not judged; they feel free to recount their own experiences and their spiritual

journey."[59] Listening to one's inner dialogue prepares the way for authentic listening to the other. Silence, reflection, and meditation allow true dialogue to occur in community.

48. Lasallian spirituality is oriented towards community.[60] It is lived together in the spirit of faith and zeal, together for mission and in "association" for the educational service of the poor. The decisive innovation of the Founder was that education is conducted within the context of community. By training and forming educators, De La Salle brought about a new community that was based on a spiritually enriched method of teaching that benefited the young, especially the poor.

49. "Fraternity and the sense of community are the greatest and the best contribution of Lasallian pedagogy to educational processes. This fraternity promotes the harmonious growth of people, helps to find meaning in life, makes it possible to create bonds of affection and solidarity, communi-

cates security and respects differences. In addition, it helps to build common dreams and transformative commitments."[61]

50. "Today, Brothers and other Lasallians discover in Association the deep meaning of Lasallian community. On the one hand, the Brothers have recovered the Vow of Association … On the other hand, all Lasallians feel called not only to share work, but also spirituality and community relationships."[62] Partners in the Lasallian mission live out a common ministry and a shared commitment to Lasallian education.  Association is "the basis of our commitment as well as the expression of our sense of belonging."[63] It is not about more work and further responsibilities, but of co-responsibility, sharing spirituality, community, and mission. It is an invitation to grow as a person and to live in fullness by developing one's own vocation in association with others. Dialogue between personal and communal experiences is the starting point for moving forward together.

51. As brothers and sisters on the journey in our individual spiritual quests, we are also spiritual companions, to one another. Our companionship is based on the richness of the fraternity that identifies us as Lasallians. We feel called to "walk together" in a shared harmony and discern our way communally and spiritually, growing in the Spirit.

Where Is Lasallian Spirituality Found?

In a Distinctive Kind of Education

52. Lasallian spirituality is a spirituality of educators and their ministry of education. It emerged from the experiences and reflections of generations of Brothers and others who adopted the pedagogical spirituality of John Baptist de La Salle. Through his example and writings, the educational movement that today encompasses many different countries, cultures, personalities, and programs is united around a set of educational principles, priorities, and beliefs that have remained consistent and long-lasting.

53. Lasallian education pays close attention to the reality of the students who are entrusted to our care, their life experiences, their human needs, their dignity as persons who seek lives of depth and meaning. Lasallian spirituality is a spirituality that is lived in daily life, in daily tasks, in the educational mission, in the Gospel imperatives, and in reading the signs of the times. It is an inclusive spirituality that is faithful and responsive to current realities, participating in the universal movement towards wholeness and wellbeing for all, and faithful and responsive to its rootedness in the Church's long tradition of educational ministry.[64]

54. De La Salle's teachers called themselves "Brothers." In defining themselves as brothers to one another and older brothers to the young people confided to them by God, they stated both their identity and their mission. This is extended today to all Lasallian educators, older brothers and sisters to their students, partners together in relationships nourished by mutual esteem, trust, respect and friendliness. It is a declaration of communion and community that animates education in a Lasallian school. Based on a lived respect for one another and for students, diversity is considered an opportunity and a gift, and therefore is recognized and embraced.[65]

55. Lasallian pedagogy places relationships at the center of its activity. Student-teacher relationships are the transformative catalysts for genuine educational success. The concrete reality of students frames the approach and content of educational accompaniment. Wherever true education happens, it is holy ground, sharing the good news of God's love and living Gospel priorities.

56. Faith is a key element in the educational encounter. "Faith not only refers to a relationship with God who acts as a 'teacher,' but it also generates a characteristic and distinctive educational relationship."[66] It informs personal and community dynamics, because we encounter God's presence in educational relationships.

In a Distinctive Kind of Educator

57. Inspired Lasallian educators are the indispensable and decisive element for the realization of Lasallian education's ends. "If there is anything that distinguishes the Lasallian proposal, since its origin, it is the dignity of the teacher, the importance assigned to their role in the educational process and the recognition of their ability to impact the character formation of the children and young people assigned to their care. ... The presence of an upright, generous, creative, and respectful teacher continues to be the primary element for the success of the Lasallian educational process."[67] The twelve virtues of a good teacher listed by St. John Baptist de La Salle succinctly summarize the qualities needed to be a Lasallian educator: Gravity, Silence, Humility, Prudence, Wisdom, Patience, Reserve, Gentleness, zeal, Vigilance, Piety, and Generosity.[68]

58. Lasallian educators, "dispensers of God's grace" among their students, are called to cultivate interiority and the spiritual dimension. Teachers educate as much by who they are as by what they do and say. "Example makes a much greater impression on the mind and the heart than words, especially for children … They are led more readily to do what they see done for them than what they hear told to them."[69] This makes it all the more important for teachers to cultivate a rich inner life and care for their personal grounding and growth. "You carry out a work that requires you to touch hearts, but this you cannot do except by the Spirit of God."[70]

59. Some educators in Lasallian schools are attracted to the richness and relevance of Lasallian spirituality; others to educational service with the poor; and still others appreciate the joy and disposition of a welcoming learning community. There is no order or hierarchy among these three pillars of Lasallian Identity. Over time, an interest in any of them tends to draw in the other two and provide a sense of unity, belonging, identity and growth.[71]

Living Lasallian Spirituality

The Personal

60. It is God's work, God's mission, that we share, and therefore it is accessible to all. It is a ministry that calls us to nourish interiority and approach each person as an expression of God's love. It is a vocation that integrates what we do and who we are in relationship to God. An active concern about one's internal growth is an ongoing concern for the inspired Lasallian educator. Personal and organized retreats, Lasallian formation programs, spiritual reading, and other intentional practices contribute to a fuller and deeper appreciation of what it means to be an inspired Lasallian educator.

61. The Lasallian heritage draws from a rich tradition of Christian reflection, yet its content and approaches are grounded in a holistic vision of the human person. Daily life is a resource for reflection and prayer, whereby one's own experiences become the means to establish a personal project. Our experiences are an invitation to open our lives to God. As we reflect and enter honestly into the day-to-day events of our lives, we become aware of God's word in them and are invited to offer ourselves to God through them.[72]

62. St. John Baptist de La Salle wrote that "The more virtue and perfection your state demands of you, the more strength and generosity you will need to achieve this."[73] The ministry of Lasallian education is a calling that benefits from prayer, genuine discernment, and generosity on the part of the educator. Practices for strengthening Lasallian spirituality include personal or interior prayer, personal meditation, spiritual retreats, community celebrations, community prayer, the Eucharist, and contact with the Scriptures and Lasallian writings.

63. Scripture, the Word of God, is a main reference point for the prayer of Lasallians. The Founder tells us "to read and to listen to the reading of Holy Scripture frequently[74] Today, as in the past, Lasallian spiritual life passes through the prayerful reading of the Word of God, quietly engaged at the personal and community level, assumed as a source of community discernment, and appropriated as part of one's own life and mission. It is necessary to listen to the Word of God and to put it into practice in order to respond to the "signs of the times" and the "movements of the Spirit." Word and life are part of the single vitality that runs through Lasallian spirituality.

64. Lasallian spirituality is a spirituality of communion and association. It is as a community that we seek, identify, and pursue the Lasallian mission and the common good, engaging all people of good will and welcoming the diverse religious experiences of those within a community. An educational community is "molded into community only through a faculty rich in the diversity and the unity of its members."[75]

The Relational

Similarly, the "gifts brought by so many people, in so many places, have enriched the Lasallian movement through the diversity of identities and vocations."[76] Relationships within a community shape the kinds of relationships that they generate within the school. It is the character of the school's adult community that models and gradually permeates the character of the larger educational community of the school. This applies to both professional, interpersonal, and Lasallian identity levels that develop over time. "The culture of a community is a determining factor in the long-term impact of organized formation experiences."[77]

65. The communal dimension of Lasallian spirituality fosters the sharing of our educational and spiritual experiences. It also supports joint pastoral activities of service. It is a spirituality of communion that generates community, a spirituality of fraternity and co-responsibility that generates commitment. Community experiences have also emerged where Partners and Brothers deepen their shared spirituality in "intentional communities" that focus on developing a deeper appreciation and understanding of their shared mission and spirituality, so that the "community becomes a visible sign of the presence of God."[78]

The Professional

66. The character, deep values, and core priorities of all those involved in a Lasallian ministry are reflected in how students are served, especially those who have greater difficulties in developing their knowledge, their skills, or themselves. When Lasallian spirituality nourishes a commitment to the poor, it becomes a spirituality of solidarity.

67. Lasallian educators are professional educators who cultivate and have acquired a sense of vocation. They are engaged in the Lasallian ministry of education and advance others when they advance themselves. St. John Baptist de La Salle described how teachers may become unbearable to their students[79] and stressed the importance of discernment. "This ought to be one of the main concerns of those who instruct others: to be able to understand their students and to discern the right way to guide them. ... This guidance requires understanding and discernment of spirits, qualities you must frequently and earnestly ask of God, because they are most necessary for you in guiding those placed in your care."[80]

Conclusion

68. The Lasallian Family is "a living reminder of God's presence in the world of education."[81] The rich gift of Lasallian spirituality is a treasure that keeps on giving and an invitation that keeps on bringing us forward. "Be satisfied with what you can do, since this satisfies God, but do not spare yourself in what you can do with the help of grace. Be convinced that, provided you are willing, you can do more with the help of God's grace than you imagine."[82]

69. The synodal process of the Church invites us to "walk together" as Lasallians, members of the People of God, to live Lasallian spirituality in depth in fraternal encounter, in listening together, in the Word of God, in prayer, in participatory spaces and in community discernment. "Together and by association" is our way of embracing Lasallian spirituality in a synodal perspective.

70. The Lasallian educational movement has been a river of grace for an untold number of students, educators, families, and others throughout its history, and it continues to be a source of growth and inspiration around the world.

Despite different cultures, backgrounds, religious traditions, or personal circumstances and challenges, the Lasallian mission keeps growing and thriving, benefiting lives in ways that remain unknown and largely hidden. It is the whispering spirit behind this core living principle of the Lasallian charism that may be called the spirituality of the Lasallian heritage, and this document is provided towards a better understanding and appreciation of that spirit.

Each person in the Lasallian Family determines how best to move forward in deepening their appreciation and understanding of what it means to be part of that Family. Along with the content provided here, we invite you to take on the challenges described in the next section on "Horizons". These are paths that draw us forward, that call for our best efforts, and that look toward a future aligned with our core Lasallian values.

3. Horizons of Lasallian Spirituality

From the riches of our Lasallian spirituality, we discern and bend our energies in the coming years to the following 5 horizon commitments for the common good.

Lasallian spirituality: **Growing deep**.

Promoters of Dialogue

3

We commit to growing a deep appreciation of the gift of difference, to be people with a heart to speak into and draw from multicultural and multi-religious realities and spiritualities, bringing an open mind, soul, and spirit.

KEY ACTIONS

Horizon Commitment 3:

- Pursue and support inter-religious, inter-faith, inter-cultural, inter-generational and other inter-dialogues.
- Live our experience of spirituality, walking together and sharing our faith with openness and synodality.
- Develop an inter-faith Lasallian spirituality, that involves members of the Lasallian Family from all religious backgrounds.

Models in Accompaniment

4 We commit to growing a deep capacity to be people who walk together in trust and compassion, whatever our individual journey, especially accompanying those most in need in today's world. This accompaniment can be done through a vibrant Lasallian community.

KEY ACTIONS

Horizon Commitment 4:

- Develop different pedagogical approaches to Lasallian spirituality adapted to different audiences and contexts.
- Establish a formal ministry and a global network of Brothers and Partners as ministers of individual and community spiritual accompaniment, who provide ways of sharing their experiences to grow deep in Lasallian identity.
- Work towards setting up a team of formators in Lasallian spirituality in each District made up of Brothers and Partners.

5 Agents of Transformation

We commit to growing towards new paths for individual and social transformation, opening the soul to the reality that we are called to follow Jesus, in whom the fully human and the fully divine are one. Such new paths widen and deepen the potential of our teaching charism to change unjust structures and relationships in the world.

KEY ACTIONS

Horizon Commitment 5:

- Develop accessible spiritual practices that are part of a daily commitment to educational ministry, personal growth and religious transformation.
- Develop, create and provide space, opportunities, activities and specific spiritual formation programs for Lasallian educators and leaders, including emerging women leaders.

Footnotes

1. Report of Lasallian Spirituality Survey (2020): https://drive.google.com/drive/folders/1vdsst-nT7vI4hoCSjIdiT81sem1wPzns?usp=sharing
2. Chapter 2 of "A Conversation for the Lasallian Family: Deepening our Identity". (Page 12 and the following) Download here. https://www.lasalle.org/wp-content/uploads/2021/03/EN_Lasallian_Family_CIAMEL_web.pdf – Online program on Lasallian Spirituality in: https://formation.lasalle.org/
3. *Lasallian Formation for Mission: The Pilgrim's Handbook* (Rome: Brothers of the Christian Schools, 2019), 133. A wider definition comes from Maria Harris: "Spirituality is our way of being in the world in the light of the Mystery at the core of the universe". Maria Harris, *Proclaim Jubilee – A Spirituality for the 21st Century* (Louisville, KY: Westminster John Knox Press, 1996), 75.
4. "Laudato Si' (24 May 2015): Pope Francis, June 18, 2015, # 91. https://www.vatican.va/content/francesco/en/encyclicals/documents/papa-francesco_20150524_enciclica-laudato-si.html (Accessed September 24, 2022.)
5. *From Hope to Commitment: Understanding Lasallian Vocations,* Circular 475 (Rome: Brothers of the Christian Schools, 2020), 27.
6. "Five Essential Marks of Catholic Schools by Archbishop J. Michael Miller, CSB." Catholic Parents OnLine, November 16, 2020. https://catholicparents.org/essential-marks-catholic-schools-archbishop-j-michael-miller-csb/ (Accessed September 24, 2022.)
7. *Lasallian Formation for Mission: The Pilgrim's Handbook* (Rome: Brothers of the Christian Schools, 2019), 132
8. *Lasallian Formation for Mission: The Pilgrim's Handbook* (Rome: Brothers of the Christian Schools, 2019), 132.
9. Rabbi Jonathan Sacks describes faith as the "belief in the objective reality of the personal. The God heard by Abraham, Moses and the prophets was not a tribal deity, group self-interest projected onto the sky. Nor was He a member of the pantheon of paganism, a capricious spirit invoked to explain why things are as they are, a pseudo-scientific construct rendered redundant by proper science. The God our ancestors heard was the voice of reality as it responds to and affirms the personal, echoing our consciousness, telling us that we are not alone. It is here, in the mystery and majesty of the personal, that God lives." Jonathan Sacks, Celebrating Life (London: Bloomsbury Continuum, an imprint of Bloomsbury Publishing Plc, 2019), 69.
10. "What Makes Education Catholic?" *Boston College Professor Thomas Groome's New Book on Catholic Education.* https://www.bc.edu/content/bc-web/bcnews/faith-religion/ministry/groome-book-what-makes-education-catholic. (Accessed September 24, 2022.)

[11] *The Catholic School on the threshold of the Third Millennium, # 9.* https://www.vatican.va/roman_curia/congregations/ccatheduc/documents/rc_con_ccatheduc_doc_27041998_school2000_en.html (Accessed September 24, 2022.)

[12] Buechner, Frederick (2004). Beyond Words: Daily Readings in the ABC's of Faith, pp. 404-405. New York: HarperCollins.

[13] *Declaration on the Lasallian Educational Mission: Challenges, Convictions, and Hopes* (Rome: Brothers of the Christian Schools, 2020), 122.

[14] De La Salle, John Baptist. *Meditations by John Baptist de La Salle*. Ed. Francis Huether and Augustine Loes, trans. Richard Arnandez (Washington, DC: Christian Brothers Conference, 1994), 437 (Med. 195.2).

[15] John Baptist de La Salle, Collection of Various Short Treatises, ed. Daniel Burke, trans. W.J. Battersby (Landover, MD: Christian Brothers Conference, 1993), 78.

[16] De La Salle, John Baptist. *Meditations by John Baptist de La Salle*. Ed. Francis Huether and Augustine Loes, trans. Richard Arnandez (Washington, DC: Christian Brothers Conference, 1994), 386 (Med. 91.2).

[17] Cf. Mark 9:38-41

[18] These were the last words that he spoke on his deathbed, when the Brother with him asked him if he accepted his sufferings. "Oui, j'adore en toutes choses la conduite de Dieu à mon égard."

[19] "The distinction between the sacred and the profane was no longer present, because everything related back to God." Bernard Hours, *Jean-Baptiste De La Salle: A Mystic in Action*, ed. George Van Grieken, trans. Anna Fitzgerald (Washington, DC: Christian Brothers Conference, 2022), 626.

[20] *Declaration on the Lasallian Educational Mission: Challenges, Convictions, and Hopes* (Rome: Brothers of the Christian Schools, 2020), 8.

[21] *Identity Criteria for the Vitality of Lasallian Educational Ministries* (Rome: Brothers of the Christian Schools, 2020), 15.

[22] *Declaration on the Lasallian Educational Mission: Challenges, Convictions, and Hopes* (Rome: Brothers of the Christian Schools, 2020), 109 (# 4.8.3). "The practice of these virtues points out pathways, encourages dreams, shows horizons, accompanies toward the achievement of autonomy, challenges, and generates mediating scenarios. The result of all these actions is the growth and personal development of the student, the empowerment of their personal capacities and solidarity with common projects." (# 4.8.3)

[23] John Johnston, "Representing Jesus Christ Himself: Identity and Hope," *1990 Pastorale Letter, 13*.

[24] "Formation for the Lasallian Mission: A Common Frame of Reference," *MEL Bulletin* 51 (April 2014), 7 (# 3.1).

[25] *Lasallian Formation for Mission: The Pilgrim's Handbook* (Rome: Brothers of the Christian Schools, 2019), 30 (# 3.2).

[26] Jean-Baptiste Blain, *The Life of John Baptist De La Salle, Founder of the Brothers of the Christian Schools,* trans. Richard Arnandez (Landover, MD: Christian Brothers Conference, 1983), Vol. 1, Bk. 1: 60-61.

[27] *From Hope to Commitment: Understanding Lasallian Vocations,* Circular 475 (Rome: Brothers of the Christian Schools, 2020), 27.

[28] *Lasallian Formation for Mission: The Pilgrim's Handbook* (Rome: Brothers of the Christian Schools, 2019), 14 (# 1.2).

[29] Hebrews 11:1

[30] *Declaration on the Lasallian Educational Mission: Challenges, Convictions, and Hopes* (Rome: Brothers of the Christian Schools, 2020), 66 (# 3.3).

[31] John Baptist de La Salle, *Religious Instructions and Exercises of Piety for the Christian Schools,* ed. Eugene Lappin, trans. Richard Arandez (Landover, MD: Christian Brothers Conference, 2002), 177.

[32] John Baptist de La Salle, *The Conduct of the Christian Schools,* ed. William Mann, trans. F. de La Fontainerie and Richard Arandez (Landover, MD: Christian Brothers Conference, 1996), 92

[33] Cf. Meds. 193.2, 197.1, 196.2, 201.2.

[34] *John Baptist de La Salle, Meditations by John Baptist De La Salle,* ed. Francis Huether and Augustine Loes, trans. Richard Arnandez (Washington, DC: Christian Brothers Conference, 1994), 437 (Med. 195.2).

[35] *The Catholic School.* The Sacred Congregation for Catholic Education. # 43. https://www.vatican.va/roman_curia/congregations/ccatheduc/documents/rc_con_ccatheduc_doc_19770319_catholic-school_en.html (Accessed September 24, 2022.)

[36] Med. 133.2

[37] Med. 80.3

[38] Med. 96.3

[39] *Declaration on the Lasallian Educational Mission: Challenges,* Convictions, and Hopes (Rome: Brothers of the Christian Schools, 2020), 78 (# 3.5.2d).

[40] Med. 37.1

[41] Med. 137.3

[42] Med. 198.1

[43] *A Conversation for the Lasallian Family:* Deepening Our Identity (Rome: Brothers of the Christian Schools, 2020), 13.

[44] "Evangelii Gaudium: Apostolic Exhortation on the Proclamation of the Gospel in Today's World" (24 November 2013), # 262. https://www.vatican.va/content/francesco/en/apost_exhortations/documents/papa-francesco_

esortazione-ap_20131124_evangelii-gaudium.html (Accessed September 24, 2022.)

[45] *A Conversation for the Lasallian Family: Deepening Our Identity* (Rome: Brothers of the Christian Schools, 2020), 14.

[46] *Declaration on the Lasallian Educational Mission: Challenges, Convictions, and Hopes* (Rome: Brothers of the Christian Schools, 2020), 88 (# 4.1).

[47] This term is from Catholic social teaching. Its expression originates from Vatican II and the document *Gaudium et Spes*.

[48] *Declaration on the Lasallian Educational Mission:* Challenges, Convictions, and Hopes (Rome: Brothers of the Christian Schools, 2020), 88-89 (# 4.1).

[49] Robert Thomas Laube, *Pentecostal Spirituality: The Lasallian Theology of Apostolic Life* (New York, NY: Desclee Company, 1970), 224.

[50] Robert Thomas Laube, *Pentecostal Spirituality: The Lasallian Theology of Apostolic Life* (New York, NY: Desclee Company, 1970), 224.

[51] *Identity Criteria for the Vitality of Lasallian Educational Ministries* (Rome: Brothers of the Christian Schools, 2020), 10.

[52] *Identity Criteria for the Vitality of Lasallian Educational Ministries* (Rome: Brothers of the Christian Schools, 2020), 17.

[53] *The Religious Dimension of Education in a Catholic School: Guidelines for Reflection and Renewal* (Congregation for Catholic Education, 1988) # 63. https://www.vatican.va/roman_curia/congregations/ccatheduc/documents/rc_con_ccatheduc_doc_19880407_catholic-school_en.html (Accessed September 24, 2022.) The end of the document states "Rome, April 7, 1988, Feast of Saint John Baptist de La Salle, Principal Patron of Teachers."

[54] "Five Essential Marks of Catholic Schools by Archbishop J. Michael Miller, CSB." Catholic Parents OnLine, November 16, 2020. https://catholicparents.org/essential-marks-catholic-schools-archbishop-j-michael-miller-csb/ (Accessed September 24, 2022.)

[55] https://www.educationglobalcompact.org/en/

[56] *Lay Catholics in School: Witnesses to Faith* (Congregation for Catholic Education, 1982), # 18.

[57] "Five Essential Marks of Catholic Schools by Archbishop J. Michael Miller, CSB." Catholic Parents OnLine, November 16, 2020. https://catholicparents.org/essential-marks-catholic-schools-archbishop-j-michael-miller-csb/ (Accessed September 24, 2022.)

[58] "Address of His Holiness Pope Francis to Participants in the 46th General Chapter of the Brothers of the Christian Schools", May 21, 2022 2022. https://www.vatican.va/content/francesco/en/speeches/2022/may/documents/20220521-fratelli-scuole-cristiane.html

[59] Pope Francis. "Homily - Opening of the Synodal Path." Opening Mass, October 10, 2021. https://www.vatican.va/content/francesco/en/

homilies/2021/documents/20211010-omelia-sinodo-vescovi.pdf

[60] *Michael Green, Now with Enthusiasm: Charism, God's Mission and Catholic Schools Today* (Mulgrave, VIC: Vaughan Publishing, 2018), 171-186.

[61] *Declaration on the Lasallian Educational Mission: Challenges, Convictions, and Hopes* (Rome: Brothers of the Christian Schools, 2020), 118.

[62] *Declaration on the Lasallian Educational Mission: Challenges, Convictions, and Hopes* (Rome: Brothers of the Christian Schools, 2020), 71.

[63] *Declaration on the Lasallian Educational Mission: Challenges, Convictions, and Hopes* (Rome: Brothers of the Christian Schools, 2020), 71.

[64] Education is described by the Church as a process that forms the whole child towards being good citizens of the world, loving God and neighbor, enriching society with the leaven of the gospel, and fulfilling their destiny to become saints. Catholic schools must transmit the full truth about the human person, created in God's image and called to life in Christ through the Holy Spirit. There is an emphasis on the dignity and the spiritual dimension of the human person. Cf. https://catholicparents.org/essential-marks-catholic-schools-archbishop-j-michael-miller-csb/ (Accessed September 24, 2022.)

[65] *Cf. Educating Today and Tomorrow: A Renewing Passion* (Congregation for Catholic Education, 2014). Vatican. (Accessed September 24, 2022.) https://www.vatican.va/roman_curia/congregations/ccatheduc/documents/rc_con_ccatheduc_doc_20140407_educare-oggi-e-domani_en.html

[66] *Declaration on the Lasallian Educational Mission: Challenges, Convictions, and Hopes* (Rome: Brothers of the Christian Schools, 2020), 67 (# 3.3.1).

[67] *Declaration on the Lasallian Educational Mission: Challenges, Convictions, and Hopes* (Rome: Brothers of the Christian Schools, 2020), 108 (# 4.8.3).

[68] John Baptist de La Salle, *Collection of Various Short Treatises,* ed. Daniel Burke, trans. W.J. Battersby (Landover, MD: Christian Brothers Conference, 1993), 5.

[69] De La Salle, John Baptist. *Meditations by John Baptist de La Salle.* Ed. Francis Huether and Augustine Loes, trans. Richard Arnandez (Washington, DC: Christian Brothers Conference, 1994), 456 (Med. 202.3).

[70] De La Salle, John Baptist. *Meditations by John Baptist de La Salle.* Ed. Francis Huether and Augustine Loes, trans. Richard Arnandez (Washington, DC: Christian Brothers Conference, 1994), 108 (Med. 43.3).

[71] *Cf. A Conversation for the Lasallian Family: Deepening Our Identity* (Rome: Brothers of the Christian Schools, 2020), 14.

[72] Cf. Schmidt, Joseph F. *Praying Our Experiences: An Invitation to Open Our Lives to God.* Frederick, MD: Word Among Us Press, 2008.

[73] De La Salle, John Baptist. *Meditations by John Baptist de La Salle.* Ed. Francis Huether and Augustine Loes, trans. Richard Arnandez (Washington, DC:

Christian Brothers Conference, 1994), 116 (Med. 49.1).

[74] De La Salle, John Baptist. *Meditations by John Baptist de La Salle*. Ed. Francis Huether and Augustine Loes, trans. Richard Arnandez (Washington, DC: Christian Brothers Conference, 1994), 185 (Med. 100.1).

[75] *The Brother of the Christian Schools in the World Today: A Declaration* (Rome: Brothers of the Christian Schools, 1967), # 46.3. Quoted in *Declaration on the Lasallian Educational Mission: Challenges, Convictions, and Hopes* (Rome: Brothers of the Christian Schools, 2020), 37 (# 1.7).

[76] *Declaration on the Lasallian Educational Mission: Challenges, Convictions, and Hopes* (Rome: Brothers of the Christian Schools, 2020), 39 (# 1.9).

[77] *Lasallian Formation for Mission: The Pilgrim's Handbook* (Rome: Brothers of the Christian Schools, 2019), 54.

[78] *Lasallian Formation for Mission: The Pilgrim's Handbook (Rome:* Brothers of the Christian Schools, 2019), 8.

[79] John Baptist de La Salle, *The Conduct of the Christian Schools,* ed. William Mann, trans. F. de La Fontainerie and Richard Arandez (Landover, MD: Christian Brothers Conference, 1996),136-137.

[80] De La Salle, John Baptist. *Meditations by John Baptist de La Salle*. Ed. Francis Huether and Augustine Loes, trans. Richard Arnandez (Washington, DC: Christian Brothers Conference, 1994), 91 (Med. 33.1).

[81] *The Rule of the Brothers of the Christian Schools* (Rome: Brothers of the Christian Schools, 2015), 61 (# 63).

[82] John Baptist de La Salle, *Collection of Various Short Treatises,* "Regarding the Use of Time," ed. Daniel Burke, trans. W.J. Battersby (Landover, MD: Christian Brothers Conference, 1993), 80.

For further resources provided through the Lasallian Resource Center, go to www.lasallianresources.org

For a virtual pilgrimage of the life of John Baptist de La Salle, go to www.dlsfootsteps.org

For information about the vocation of the Brothers of the Christian Schools, go to www.brothersvocation.org

This is a publication by the Lasallian Resource Center, which is part of the Christian Brothers Conference (CBC), the office for the Lasallian Region of North America (RELAN) for the Brothers of the Christian Schools. (www.lasallian.info)

Notes

Notes

Notes

Notes

Made in the USA
Middletown, DE
17 April 2024